Zuñi Coyote Tales

Zuñi

Coyote

Tales

COMPILED BY

FRANK HAMILTON CUSHING

THE UNIVERSITY

OF ARIZONA PRESS

TUCSON

The stories included in this book are reprinted from *Zuñi Folk Tales*, by Frank Hamilton Cushing (1901; University of Arizona Press, 1986).

The University of Arizona Press
© 1998 The Arizona Board of Regents

LIBRARY OF CONGRESS CATALOGING-IN-PUBLICATION DATA
Cushing, Frank Hamilton, 1857–1900.
[Zuñi folk tales]
Zuñi coyote tales/compiled by Frank Hamilton Cushing.
p.   cm.
Originally published: Zuñi folk tales: New York: Putnam, 1901.
ISBN 0-8165-1892-0 (pbk.)
1. Zuni Indians—Folklore. 2. Coyote (Legendary character)—
Legends. I. Title
E99.Z9C92   1998   97-51899
398.2'089'979–dc21

Manufactured in the United States of America on acid-free, archival-quality paper.

19 18 17   8 7 6 5

CONTENTS

Zuñi Coyote Tales

*H*ow the Coyote Joined the

Dance of the Burrowing-Owls

*Y*ou may know the country that lies south of the valley in which our town stands. You travel along the trail which winds round the hill our ancients called *Ishana-tak'yapon*— which means the Hill of Grease, for the rocks sometimes shine in the light of the sun at evening, and it is said that strange things occurred there in the days of the ancients, which makes them thus to shine, while rocks of the kind in other places do not—you travel on up this trail, crossing over the arroyos and foot-hills of the great mesa called Middle Mountain, until you come to the foot of the cliffs. Then you climb up back and forth, winding round and round, until you reach the top of the mountain, which is as flat as the floor of a house, merely being here and there traversed by small valleys covered with piñon and cedar, and threaded by trails made not only by the feet of our people but by deer and other animals. And so you go on and on, until, hardly knowing it, you have descended from the top of Middle Mountain, and found yourself in a wide plain covered with grass, and here and there clumps of trees. Beyond this valley is an elevated sandy plain, rather sunken in the middle, so that when it rains the water filters down into the soil of the depressed portion (which is wide enough to be a country in itself) and nourishes the grasses there; so that most of the year they grow green and sweet.

Now, a long, long time ago, in this valley or basin there lived a village of Prairie-dogs, on fairly peaceable terms with Rattlesnakes, Adders, Chameleons, Horned-toads, and Burrowing-owls. With the Owls they were especially friendly, looking at them as creatures of great gravity and sanctity. For this reason these Prairie-dogs and their companions never disturbed the councils or ceremonies of the Burrowing-owls, but treated them most respectfully, keeping at a distance from them when their dances were going on.

It chanced one day that the Burrowing-owls were having a great dance all to themselves, rather early in the morning. The dance they were engaged in was one peculiarly prized by them, requiring no little dexterity in its execution. Each dancer, young man or maiden, carried upon his or her head a bowl of foam, and though their legs were crooked and their motions disjointed, they danced to the whistling of some and the clapping beaks of others, in perfect unison, and with such dexterity that they never spilled a speck of the foam on their sleek mantles of dun-black feather-work.

It chanced this morning of the Foam-dance that a Coyote was nosing about for Grasshoppers and Prairie-dogs. So quite naturally he was prowling around the by-streets in the borders of the Prairie-dog town. His house where he lived with his old grandmother stood back to the westward, just over the elevations that bounded Sunken Country, among the rocks. He heard the click-clack of the musicians and their shrill, funny little song:

> I yami hota utchu tchapikya,
>   Tokos! tokos! tokos! tokos!

So he pricked up his ears, and lifting his tail, trotted forward toward the level place between the hillocks and doorways of the village, where the Owls were dancing in a row. He looked at them with great curiosity, squatting on his haunches, the more composedly to observe them. Indeed, he became so much interested and amused by their shambling motions and clever evolutions, that he could no longer contain his curiosity. So he stepped forward, with a smirk and a nod toward the old master of ceremonies, and said: "My father, how are you and your children these many days?"

"Contented and happy," replied the old Owl, turning his attention to the dancing again.

"Yes, but I observe you are dancing," said the Coyote. "A very fine dance, upon my word! Charming! Charming! And why should you be dancing if you were not contented and happy, to be sure?"

"We are dancing," responded the Owl, "both for our pleasure and for the good of the town."

"True, true," replied the Coyote; "but what's that which looks like foam these dancers are carrying on their heads, and why do they dance in so limping a fashion?"

"You see, my friend," said the Owl, turning toward the Coyote, "we hold this to be a very sacred performance—very sacred indeed. Being such, these my children are initiated and so trained in the mysteries of the sacred society of which this is a custom that they can do very strange things in the observance of our ceremonies. You ask what it is that looks like foam they are balancing on their heads. Look more closely, friend. Do you not observe that it is their own grandmothers' heads they have on, the feathers turned white with age?"

"By my eyes!" exclaimed the Coyote, blinking and twitching his whiskers; "it seems so."

"And you ask also why they limp as they dance," said the Owl. "Now, this limp is essential to the proper performance of our dance—so essential, in fact, that in order to attain to it these my children go through the pain of having their legs broken. Instead of losing by this, they gain in a great many ways. Good luck always follows them. They are quite as spry as they were before, and enjoy, moreover, the distinction of performing a dance which no other people or creatures in the world are capable of!"

"Dust and devils!" ejaculated the Coyote. "This is passing strange. A most admirable dance, upon my word! Why, every bristle on my body keeps time to the music and their steps! Look here, my friend, don't you think that I could learn that dance?"

"Well," replied the old Owl; "it is rather hard to learn, and you haven't been initiated, you know; but, still, if you are determined that you would like to join the dance—by the way, have you a grandmother?"

"Yes, and a fine old woman she is," said he, twitching his mouth in the direction of his house. "She lives there with me. I dare say she is looking after my breakfast now."

"Very well," continued the old Owl, "if you care to join in our dance, fulfill the conditions, and I think we can receive you into our order." And he added, aside: "The silly fool; the sneaking, impertinent wretch! I will teach him to be sticking that sharp nose of his into other people's affairs!"

"All right! All right!" cried the Coyote, excitedly. "Will it last long?"

"Until the sun is so bright that it hurts our eyes," said the Owl; "a long time yet."

"All right! All right! I'll be back in a little while," said the Coyote; and, switching his tail into the air, away he ran toward his home. When he came to the house, he saw his old grandmother on the roof, which was a rock beside his hole, gathering fur from some skins which he had brought home, to make up a bed for the Coyote's family.

"Ha, my blessed grandmother!" said the Coyote, "by means of your aid, what a fine thing I shall be able to do!"

The old woman was singing to herself when the Coyote dashed up to the roof where she was sitting, and, catching up a convenient leg-bone, whacked her over the pate and sawed her head off with the teeth of a deer. All bloody and soft as it was, he clapped it on his own head and raised himself on his hind-legs, bracing his tail against the ground, and letting his paws drop with the toes outspread, to imitate as nearly as possible the drooping wings of the dancing Owls. He found that it worked very well; so descending with the head in one paw and a stone in the other, he found a convenient sharp-edged rock, and laying his legs across it, hit them a tremendous crack with the stone, which broke them to be sure, into splinters.

"Beloved Powers! Oh!" howled the Coyote. "Oh-o-o-o-o! the dance may be a fine thing, but the initiation is anything else!"

However, with his faith unabated, he shook himself together and got up to walk. But he could walk only with his paws; his hind-legs dragged helplessly behind him. Nevertheless, with great pain, and getting weaker and weaker every step of the way, he made what haste he could back to the Prairie-dog town, his poor old grandmother's head slung over his shoulders.

When he approached the dancers—for they were still

dancing—they pretended to be greatly delighted with their proselyte, and greeted him, notwithstanding his rueful countenance, with many congratulatory epithets, mingled with very proper and warm expressions of welcome. The Coyote looked sick and groaned occasionally and kept looking around his feet, as though he would like to lick them. But the old Owl extended his wing and cautioned him not to interfere with the working power of faith in this essential observance, and invited him (with a *HEM* that very much resembled a suppressed giggle), to join in their dance. The Coyote smirked and bowed and tried to stand up gracefully on his stumps, but fell over, his grandmother's head rolling around in the dirt. He picked up the grisly head, clapped it on his crown again and raised himself, and with many a howl, which he tried in vain to check, began to prance around; but ere long tumbled over again. The Burrowing-owls were filled with such merriment at his discomfiture that they laughed until they spilled the foam all down their backs and bosoms; and, with a parting fling at the Coyote which gave him to understand that he had made a fine fool of himself, and would know better than to pry into other people's business next time, skipped away to a safe distance from him.

Then, seeing how he had been tricked, the Coyote fell to

howling and clapping his thighs; and, catching sight of his poor grandmother's head, all bloody and begrimed with dirt, he cried out in grief and anger: "Alas! Alas! that it should have come to this! You little devils! I'll be even with you! I'll smoke you out of your holes."

"What will you smoke us out with?" tauntingly asked the Burrowing-owls.

"Ha! you'll find out. With yucca!"

"O! O! ha! ha!" laughed the Owls. "That is our succotash!"

"Ah, well! I'll smoke you out!" yelled the Coyote, stung by their taunt.

"What with?" cried the Owls.

"Grease-weed."

"He, ha! ho, ho! We make our mush-stew of that!"

"Ha, but I'll smoke you out, nevertheless, you little beasts!"

"What with? What with?" shouted the Owls.

"Yellow-top weeds," said he.

"Ha, ha! All right; smoke away! We make our sweet gruel with that, you fool!"

"I'll fix you! I'll smoke you out! I'll suffocate the very last one of you!"

"What with? What with?" shouted the Owls, skipping around on their crooked feet.

"Pitch-pine," snarled the Coyote.

This frightened the Owls, for pitch-pine, even to this day, is sickening to them. Away they plunged into their holes, pell-mell.

Then the Coyote looked at his poor old grandmother's begrimed and bloody head, and cried out—just as Coyotes do now at sunset, I suppose—"Oh, my poor, poor grandmother! So this is what they have caused me to do to you!" And, tormented both by his grief and his pain, he took up the head of his grandmother and crawled back as best he could to his house.

When he arrived there he managed to climb up to the roof, where her body lay stiff. He chafed her legs and sides, and washed the blood and dirt from her head, and got a bit of sinew, and sewed her head to her body as carefully as he could and as hastily. Then he opened her mouth, and putting his muzzle to it, blew into her throat, in the hope of resuscitating her; but the wind only leaked out from the holes in her neck, and she gave no signs of animation. Then the Coyote mixed some pap of fine toasted meal and water and poured it down her throat, addressing her with vehement expressions of regret at what he had done, and apology and solicitation that she should not mind, as he didn't mean it, and imploring her to revive. But the pap only trickled out between the stitches in her neck, and she grew colder and stiffer all the while; so that at last the Coyote gave it up, and, moaning, he betook himself to a near clump of piñon trees, intent upon vengeance and designing to gather pitch with which to smoke the Owls to death. But, weakened by his injuries, and filled with grief and shame and mortification, when he got there he could only lie down.

He was so engrossed in howling and thinking of his woes and pains that a Horned-toad, who saw him, and who hated him because of the insults he had frequently suffered from him and his kind, crawled into the throat of the beast without his noticing it. Presently the little creature struck up a song:

> Tsakina muuu-ki
> Iyami Kushina tsoiyakya
> Aisiwaiki muki, muki,
> Muuu ka!

"Ah-a-a-a-a-a," the Coyote was groaning. But when he heard this song, apparently far off, and yet so near, he felt very strangely inside, so he thought and no doubt wondered if it were the song of some musician. At any rate, he lifted his head and looked all around, but hearing nothing, lay down again and bemoaned his fate.

Then the Horned-toad sang again. This time the Coyote called out immediately, and the Horned-toad answered: "Here I am." But look as he would, the Coyote could not find the Toad. So he listened for the song again, and heard it, and asked who it was that was singing. The Horned-toad replied that it was he. But still the Coyote could not find him. A fourth time the Horned-toad sang, and the Coyote began to suspect that it was under him. So he lifted himself to see; and one of the spines on the Horned-toad's neck pricked him, and at the same time the little fellow called out: "Here I am, you idiot, inside of you! I came upon you here, and being a medicine-man of some prominence, I thought I would explore your vitals and see what was the matter."

"By the souls of my ancestors!" exclaimed the Coyote, "be careful what you do in there!"

The Horned-toad replied by laying his hand on the Coyote's liver, and exclaiming: "What is this I feel?"

"Where?" said the Coyote.

"Down here."

"Merciful daylight! It is my liver, without which no one can have solidity of any kind, or a proper vitality. Be very careful not to injure that; if you do, I shall die at once, and what will become of my poor wife and children?"

Then the Horned-toad climbed up to the stomach of the Coyote. "What is this, my friend?" said he, feeling the sides of the Coyote's food-bag.

"What is it like?" asked the Coyote.

"Wrinkled," said the Horned-toad, "and filled with a fearful mess of stuff!"

"Oh! mercy! mercy! good daylight! My precious friend, be very careful! That is the very source of my being—my stomach itself!"

"Very well," said the Horned-toad. Then he moved on somewhat farther and touched the heart of the Coyote, which startled him fearfully. "What is this?" cried the Horned-toad.

"Mercy, mercy! what are you doing?" explained the Coyote.

"Nothing—feeling of your vitals," was the reply. "What is it?"

"Oh, what is it like?" said the Coyote.

"Shaped like a pine-nut," said the Horned-toad, "as nearly as I can make out; it keeps leaping so."

"Leaping, is it?" howled the Coyote. "Mercy! my friend, get away from there! That is the very heart of my being, the thread that ties my existence, the home of my emotions, and my knowledge of daylight. Go away from there, do, I pray you! If you should scratch it ever so little, it would be the death of me, and what would my wife and children do?"

"Hey!" said the Horned-toad, "you wouldn't be apt to insult me and my people anymore if I touched you up there a little, would you?" And he hooked one of his horns into the Coyote's heart.

The Coyote gave one gasp, straightened out his limbs, and expired.

"Ha, ha! you villain! Thus would you have done to me, had you found the chance; thus unto you"—saying which he found his way out and sought the nearest water-pocket he could find.

So you see from this, which took place in the days of the ancients, it may be inferred that the instinct of meddling with everything that did not concern him, and making a universal nuisance of himself, and desiring to imitate everything that he sees, ready to jump into any trap that is laid for him, is a confirmed instinct with the Coyote, for those are precisely his characteristics today.

Furthermore, Coyotes never insult Horned-toads nowadays, and they keep clear of Burrowing-owls. And ever since then the Burrowing-owls have been speckled with gray and white all over their backs and bosoms, because their ancestors spilled foam over themselves in laughing at the silliness of the Coyote.

Thus shortens my story.

The Coyote Who Killed

the Demon Síuiuki

or,

Why Coyotes Run Their

Noses into Deadfalls

*I*t was very long ago, in the days of the ancients. There
stood a village in the cañon south of Thunder Mountain where
the Gods of Prey all lived with their sisters and mothers: the
Mountain Lion, the great Black Bear, the Wildcat, the Gray
Wolf, the Eagle, and even the Mole—all the Gods of Prey lived
there together with their mothers and sisters. Day after day they
went out hunting, for hunting was their business of life, and
they were great hunters.

Now, right up on the edge of Thunder Mountain there
lived a spotted Demon, named Síuiuki, and whenever the
people of the towns round about went hunting, he lay in wait
for them and ate them up.

After a long while the Gods of Prey grew discontented,

and they said to one another: "What in the world can we do? None of the children of men ever make sacrifices to us, for, whenever our children among men go out hunting, this Demon who lives on the top of Thunder Mountain destroys them and eats them up. What in the world can be done?"

"It would be a good thing if we could kill him," said some of them.

Now, just down below the house of the Demon, in Wolf Cañon, lived a Coyote, and he had found out where the Gods of Prey lived, and whenever he wanted a feast of sinew and gristle, he went below their houses and gnawed at the bones that they had thrown away, and thus it happened that when the gods were talking together in this way he was near their doorway gnawing a bone, and he heard all they said.

"Yes," said one or two of the others, "and if anybody will go and kill Síuiuki, we will give him our sister to marry."

"Aha!" said the Coyote to himself. "Ha, ha!"—and he dropped the bone he was gnawing and cut off for home as fast as ever he could.

Next morning, bright and early, he began to dig into the side of the cañon below the Demon's home, and after he had dug a great hollow in the side of the arroyo, he rolled a heavy stone into it, and found another, which he placed beside it. Then he brought a great many leg-bones of deer and antelope. Then he found a large bowl and put a lot of yellow medicine-fluid in it, and placed it beside the rock. He then sat down and began to crack the leg-bones with the two stones he had brought there.

The old Demon was not in the habit of rising very early, but when he arose that morning he came out and sat down on the edge of the cliff; there the Coyote was, battering away at the bones and pretending to bathe his own lips with the medicine-fluid.

"I wonder what in the world that little sneak is doing down there," said the old Demon. So he put on his war-badge and took his bow and arrows, as though he was going out to hunt, and started down to where the Coyote was.

"Hello!" said the Coyote, "how did you pass the night?"

"What in the world are you doing here?" asked the Demon.

"Why, don't you know?" replied the Coyote. "This is the way I train myself for running, so as to catch the deer; I can run faster than any deer in the country. With my medicine, here, I take the swiftness out of these bones."

"Is it possible?" said the old Demon.

"Of course it is," said the Coyote. "There is no deer that can run away from me."

"Will you show me?" said the Demon, eagerly.

"Why, yes, of course I will; and then we will go hunting together."

"Good, good!" said the old Demon. "I have a hard time catching deer and antelope."

"Well, now, you sit down right over there and watch me," said the Coyote, "and I will show you all about it."

So he laid his left leg over the rock, and then slily took an antelope bone and laid it by the side of it. Then he picked up a large stone and struck it as hard as ever he could against the bone. Whack! went the stone, and it split the bone into splinters; and the Coyote pretended that it was the bone of his own leg.

"Aye! Ah! Oh!" exclaimed he. "But then it will get well!" Still crying "Oh! Ah!" he splashed the leg with the medicine-water and rubbed it. "Didn't I tell you?" said he, "it is all right now." And then away he went and ran like lightning round and round on the plain below, and rushed back again. "Didn't I tell you so?" said he.

"Fury! what a runner it makes out of you," said the old

Demon, and his eyes stuck out more than ever. "Let me try it now."

"Hold on, hold on," said the Coyote; "I have not half finished yet."

So he repeated the experiment with his other leg, and made great ado, as if it hurt him more than ever. But, pretending to cure himself with the medicine-water, he ran round and round on the plain below so fast that he fairly left a streak of dust behind him.

"Why, indeed, you are one of the fastest runners I ever saw!" said the Demon, rubbing his eyes.

Then the Coyote repeated the experiment first with his left paw and then with his right; and the last time he ran more swiftly than before.

"Why, do you mean to say that if I do that I can run as fast as you do?" said the Demon.

"Certainly," replied the Coyote. "But it will hurt you."

"Ho! who cares for a little hurt?" said the Demon.

"Oh! but it hurts terribly," said the Coyote, "and I am afraid you won't have the pluck to go through with it."

"Do you think I am a baby?" said the old Demon, getting up—"or a woman, that I should be afraid to pound my legs and arms?"

"Well, I only thought I'd tell you how much it hurts," said the Coyote; "but if you want to try it yourself, why, go ahead. There's one thing certain: when you make yourself as swift as I am, there's no deer in all the country that can get away from us two."

"What shall I do?" said the Demon.

"You just sit right down there, and I'll show you how," said the Coyote. So the Demon sat down by the rock.

"There, now, you just lay your leg right over that stone and take the other rock and strike your leg just as hard as you can; and as soon as you have done, bathe it in the medicine-water. Then do just the same way to the other."

"All right," said the Demon. So he laid his leg over the rock, and picking up the other stone, brought it down with might and main across his thigh—so hard, indeed, that he crushed the bone into splinters.

"Oh, my! On, my! what shall I do?" shouted the Demon.

"Be patient, be patient; it will get well," said the Coyote, and he splashed it with the medicine-fluid.

Then, picking up the stone again, the Demon hit the other thigh even harder, from pain.

"It will get well, my friend; it will get well," shouted the

Coyote; and he splashed more of the medicine-water on the two wounded legs.

Then the Demon picked up the stone once more, and, laying his left arm across the other stone, pounded that also until it was broken.

"Hold on; let me bathe it for you," said the Coyote. "Does it hurt? Oh, well, it will get well. Just wait until you have doctored the other arm, and then in a few minutes you will be all right."

"Oh, dear! Oh, dear!" groaned the Demon. "How in the world can I doctor the other arm, for my left arm is broken?"

"Lay it across the rock, my friend," said the Coyote, "and I'll doctor it for you."

So the Demon did as he was bidden, and the Coyote brought the stone down with might and main against his arm. "Have patience, my friend, have patience," said he, as he bathed the injured limb with more of the medicine-water. But the Demon only groaned and howled, and rolled over and over in the dust with pain.

"Ha, ha!" laughed the Coyote, as he keeled a somersault over the rocks and ran off over the plain. "How do you feel now, old man?"

"But it hurts! It hurts!" cried the Demon. "I shall never get well; it will kill me!"

"Of course it will," laughed the Coyote. "That's just what I wanted it to do, you old fool!"

So the old Demon lay down and died from sheer pain.

Then the Coyote took the Demon's knife from him, and cutting open his breast, tore out his heart, wind-pipe, and all. Then, stealing the war-badge that the Demon had worn, he cut away as fast as ever he could for the home of the Prey-gods. Before noon he neared their house, and, just as he ran up into the plaza in front of it, the youngest sister of the Prey-gods came out to hang up some meat to dry. Now, her brothers had all gone hunting; not one of them was at home.

"I say, wife," said the Coyote. "Wife! Wife!"

"Humph!" said the girl. "Impertinent scoundrel! I wonder where he is and who he is that has the impudence to call me his wife when he knows that I have never been married!"

"Wife! Wife!" shouted the Coyote again.

"Away with you, you shameless rascal!" cried the girl, in indignation. Then she looked around and spied the Coyote sitting there on the ash-heap, with his nose in the air, as though he were the biggest fellow in the world.

"Clear out, you wretch!" cried the girl.

"Softly, softly," replied the Coyote. "Do you remember what your brothers said last night?"

"What was that?" said the girl.

"Why, whoever would kill the speckled Demon, they declared, should have you for his wife."

"Well, what of that?" asked the girl.

"Oh, nothing," replied the Coyote, "only I've killed him!" And, holding up the Demon's heart and war-badge, he stuck his nose in the air again.

So the poor girl said not a word, but sat there until the Coyote called out: "I say, wife, come down and take me up; I can't climb the ladders."

So the poor girl went down the ladder, took her foul-smelling husband in her arms, and climbed up with him.

"Now, take me in with you," said the Coyote. So she did as she was bidden. Then she was about to mix some dough, but the Coyote kept getting in her way.

"Get out of the way a minute, won't you?" said the girl, "until I cook something for you."

"I want you to come and sit down with me," said the Coyote, "and let me kiss you, for you know you are my wife, now." So the poor girl had to submit to the ill-smelling creature's embraces.

Presently along came her brother, the Gray Wolf, but he was a very good-natured sort of fellow; so he received the Coyote pleasantly. Then along came the Bear, with a big antelope over his shoulder; but he didn't say anything, for he was a lazy, good-natured fellow. Then presently the other brothers came in, one by one; but the Mountain Lion was so late in returning that they began to look anxiously out for him. When they saw him coming from the north with more meat and more game than all the others together had brought, he was evidently not in good humor, for as he approached the house he exclaimed, with a howl: "*Hu-hu-ya!*"

"There he goes again," said the brothers and sisters, all in a chorus. "Always out of temper with something."

"*Hu-hu-ya!*" exclaimed the Mountain Lion again, louder than before. And, as he mounted the ladder, he exclaimed for a third time: "*Hu-hu-ya!*" and, throwing his meat down, entered swearing and growling until his brothers were ashamed of him, and told him he had better behave himself.

"Come and eat," said the sister, as she brought a bowl of meat and put it on the floor.

"*Hu-hu-ya!*" again exclaimed the Mountain Lion, as he came nearer and sat down to eat. "What in the world is the matter with you sister? You smell just like a Coyote. *Hu-hu-ya!*"

"Have you no more decency than to come home and scold your sister in that way?" exclaimed the Wolf. "I'm disgusted with you."

"*Hu-hu-ya!*" reiterated the Mountain Lion.

Now, when the Coyote had heard the Mountain Lion coming, he had sneaked off into a corner; but he stuck his sharp nose out, and the Mountain Lion espied it. "*Hu-hu-ya!*" said he. "Sling that bad-smelling beast out of the house! Kick him out!" cried the old man, with a growl. So the sister, fearing that her brother would eat her husband up, took the Coyote in her arms and carried him into another room.

"Now, stay there and keep still, for brother is very cross; but then he is always cross if things don't go right," she said.

So when evening came her brothers began to discuss where they would go hunting the next day; and the Coyote, who was listening at the door, heard them. So he called out: "Wife! Wife!"

"*Shom-me!*" remarked old Long Tail. "Shut up, you dirty whelp." And as the sister arose to go to see what her husband wanted, the Mountain Lion remarked: "You had better sling that foul-smelling cub of yours over the roof."

No sooner had the girl entered than the Coyote began to brag what a runner he was, and to cut around at a great rate.

"*Shom-me!*" exclaimed the Mountain Lion again. "A Coyote always will make a Coyote of himself, foul-smelling wretch! *Hu-hu-ya!*"

"Shut up, and behave yourself!" cried the Wolf. "Don't you know any better than to talk about your brother-in-law in that way?" But neither the Coyote nor the girl could sleep that night for the growlings and roarings of their big brother, the Long Tail.

When the brothers began to prepare for the hunt the next morning, out came the Coyote all ready to accompany them. "You, you?" said the Mountain Lion. "You going to hunt with us? You conceited sneak!"

"Let him go if he wants to," said the Wolf.

"*Hu-hu-ya!* Fine company!" remarked the Mountain Lion. "If you fellows want to walk with him, you may. There's one thing certain, I'll not be seen in his company," and away strode the old fellow, lashing his tail and growling as he went. So the Coyote, taking a luncheon of dried meat that his wife put up for him, sneaked along behind with his tail dragging in the dust. Finally they all reached the mountain where they intended to hunt, and soon the Mountain Lion and the Bear started out to drive in a herd of antelope that they had scented in the distance. Presently along rushed the leaders of the herd.

"Now, then, I'll show your cross old brother whether I can hunt or not," cried the Coyote, and away he rushed right into the herd of antelope and deer before anyone could restrain him. Of course he made a Coyote of himself, and away went the deer in all directions. Nevertheless, the brothers, who were great hunters, succeeded in catching a few of them; and, just as they sat down to lunch, the Mountain Lion returned with a big elk on his shoulders.

"Where is our sweet-scented brother-in-law?" he asked.

"Nobody knows," replied they. "He rushed off after the deer and antelope, and that was the last of him."

"Of course the beast will make a Coyote of himself. But he can go till he can go no longer, for all I care," added the Mountain Lion, as he sat down to eat.

Presently along came the Coyote.

"Where's your game, my fine hunter?" asked the Mountain Lion.

"They all got away from me," whined the Coyote.

"Of course they did, you fool!" sneered the Mountain Lion. "The best thing that you can do is to go home and see your wife. Here, take this meat to sister," said he, slinging him a haunch of venison.

"Where's the road?" asked the Coyote.

"Well," said the Wolf, "follow that path right over there until you come to where it forks; then be sure to take the right-hand trail, for if you follow the left-hand trail it will lead you away from home and into trouble."

"Which trail did you say?" cried the Coyote.

"*Shom-me!*" again exclaimed the Mountain Lion.

"Oh, yes," hastily added the Coyote; "the right-hand trail. No, the left-hand trail."

"Just what you might expect," growled the Mountain Lion. "Already the fool has forgotten what you told him. Well, as for me, he can go on the left-hand trail if he wants to, and the farther he goes the better."

"Now, be sure and take the right-hand trail," called the Wolf, as the coyote started.

"I know, I know," cried the Coyote; and away he went with his heavy haunch of venison slung over his shoulder. After a while he came to the fork in the trail. "Let me see," said he, "it's the left-hand trail, it seems to me. No, the right-hand trail. Well, I declare, I've forgotten! Perhaps it is the right-hand trail, and maybe it is the left-hand trail. Yes, it is the left-hand trail. Now I'm certain." And picking up his haunch of venison, away he trotted along the left-hand trail. Presently he came to a steep cliff and began to climb it. But he had no sooner reached the middle than a lot of Chimney-swallows began to fly around his head and pick at his eyes, and slap him on the nose with their wings.

"Oh, dear! oh, dear!" exclaimed the Coyote. "Aye! aye!" and he bobbed his head from side to side to dodge the Swallows, until he missed his footing, and down he tumbled, heels over head—meat, Coyote, and all—until he struck a great pile of rocks below, and was dashed to pieces.

That was the end of the Coyote; but not of my story.

Now, the brothers went on hunting again. Then, one by one, they returned home. As before, the Mountain Lion came in last of all. He smelt all about the room. "Whew!" exclaimed he. "It still smells here as if twenty Coyotes had been around. But it seems to me that our fine brother-in-law isn't anywhere about."

"No," responded the rest, with troubled looks on their

faces. "Nobody has seen anything of him yet."

"*Shom—m-m!*" remarked the Mountain Lion again. "Didn't I tell you, brothers, that he was a fool and would forget your directions? I say I told you that before he started. Well, for my part, I hope the beast has gone so far that he will never return," and with that he ate his supper.

When supper was over, the sister said: "Come brothers, let's go and hunt for my husband."

At first the Mountain Lion growled and swore a great deal; but at last he consented to go. When they came to where the trails forked, there were the tracks of the Coyote on the left-hand trail.

"The idiot!" exclaimed the Mountain Lion. "I hope he has fallen off the cliff and broken every bone in his body!"

When at last the party reached the mountain, sure enough, there lay the body of the Coyote, with not a whole bone in him except his head.

"Good enough for you," growled the Mountain Lion, as he picked up a great stone and, *tu-um!* threw it down with all his strength upon the head of the Coyote.

That's what happened a great while ago. And for that

reason whenever a Coyote sees a bait of meat inside of a stone deadfall he is sure to stick his nose in and get his head mashed for his pains.

Thus shortens my story.

How the Coyotes Tried to Steal

the Children of the Sacred Dance

*I*n the times of the ancients, when our people lived in various places about the valley of Zuñi where ruins now stand, it is said that an old Coyote lived in Cedar Cañon with his family, which included a fine litter of pups. It is also said that at this time there lived on the crest of Thunder Mountain, back of the broad rock column or pinnacle which guards its western portion, one of the gods of the Sacred Drama Dance (*Kâkâ*),[1] named K'yámakwe, with his children, many in number and altogether like himself.

One day the old Coyote of Cedar Cañon went out hunting, and as he was prowling around among the sage-bushes below Thunder Mountain, he heard the clang and rattle and the shrill cries of the K'yámakwe. He pricked up his ears, stuck his nose into the air, sniffed about and looked all around, and presently discovered the K'yámakwe children running rapidly back and forth on the very edge of the mountain.

"Delight of my senses, what pretty creatures they are! Good for me!" he piped, in a jovial voice. "I am the finder of children. I must capture the little fellows tomorrow, and bring them up as Coyotes ought to be brought up. Aren't they handsome, though?"

All this he said to himself, in a fit of conceit, with his nose in the air (presumptuous cur!), planning to steal the children of a god! He hunted no more that day, but ran home as fast as he could, and, arriving there, he said: "Wife! Wife! O wife! I have discovered a number of the prettiest waifs one ever saw. They are children of the *Kâkâ*, but what matters that? They are there, running back and forth and clanging their rattles along the very edge of Thunder Mountain. I mean to steal them tomorrow, everyone of them, and bring them here!"

"Mercy on us!" exclaimed the old Coyote's wife. "There are children enough and to spare already. What in the world can we do with all of them, you fool?"

"But they are pretty," said the Coyote. "Immensely fine! Every Coyote in the country would envy us the possession of them!"

"But you say they are many," continued the wife.

"Well, yes, a good many," said the Coyote.

"Well, why not divide them among our associated clans?" suggested the old woman. "You never can capture them alone; it is rare enough that you capture *anything* alone, leave out the children of the K'yámakwe. Get your relatives to help you, and divide the children amongst them."

"Well, now, come to think of it, it is a good plan," said the Coyote, with his nose on his neck. "If I get up this expedition I'll be a big chief, won't I? Hurrah! Here's for it!" he shouted; and, switching his tail in the face of his wife, he shot out of the hole and ran away to a high rock, where, squatting down with a most important air and his nose lifted high, he cried out:

Au hii lâ-â-â-â!
> *Su Homaya-kwe!*
> *Su Kemaya-kwe!*
> *Su Ayalla-kwe!*
> *Su Kutsuku-kwe!*
[Listen ye all!
> Coyotes of the Cedar-cañon tribe!
> Coyotes of the Sunflower-stalk-plain tribe!
> Coyotes of the Lifted-stone-mountain tribe!
> Coyotes of the Place-of-rock-gullies tribe!]

I have instructions for you this day. I have found waif
children many—of the K'yámakwe, the young. I would steal the
waif-children many, of the K'yámakwe, the young. I would steal
them tomorrow, that they may be adopted of us. I would have
your aid in the stealing of the K'yámakwe young. Listen ye all,
and tomorrow gather in council. Thus much I instruct ye:

Coyotes of the Cedar-cañon tribe!
Coyotes of the Sunflower-stalk-plain tribe!
Coyotes of the Lifted-stone-mountain tribe!
Coyotes of the Place-of-rock-gullies tribe!

It was growing dark, and immediately from all quarters, in
dark places under the cañons and arroyos, issued answering
howls and howls. You should have seen that crowd of Coyotes
the next morning, large and small, old and young—all four
tribes gathered together in the plain below Thunder Mountain!

When they had all assembled, the Coyote who had made
the discovery mounted an ant-hill, sat down, and, lifting his paw,
was about to give directions with the air of a chief when an ant
bit him. He lost his dignity, but resumed it again on the top of a
neighboring rock. Again he stuck his nose into the air and his
paw out, and with ridiculous assumption informed the Coyotes

that he was chief of them all and that they would do well to pay attention to his directions. He then showed himself much more skillful than you might have expected. As you know, the cliff of Thunder Mountain is very steep, especially that part back of the two standing rocks. Well, this was the direction of the Coyote:

"One of you shall place himself at the base of the mountain; another shall climb over him, and the first one shall grasp his tail; and another over them, and his tail shall be grasped by the second, and so on until the top is reached. Hang tight my friends, every one of you, and every one fall in line. Eructate thoroughly before you do so. If you do not, we may be in a pretty mess; for supposing that any one along the line should hiccough, he would lose his hold, and down we would all fall!"

So the Coyotes all at once began to curve their necks and swell themselves up and strain and wriggle and belch wind as much as possible. Then all fell into a line and grabbed each other's tails, and thus they extended themselves in a long string up the very face of Thunder Mountain. A ridiculous little pup was at one end and a good, strong, grizzled old fellow—no other than the chief of the party—at the other.

"Souls of my ancestors! Hang tight, my friends! Hang tight!" said he, when, suddenly, one near the top, in the agitation of the moment, began to sneeze, lost his hold, and down the whole string, hundreds of them, fell, and were completely flattened out among the rocks.

The warrior of the *Kâkâ*—he of the Long Horn, with frightful, staring eyes, and visage blue with rage—bow and war-club in hand, was hastening from the sacred lake in the west to rescue the children of the K'yámakwe. When he arrived they had been rescued already, so, after storming around a little and mauling such of the Coyotes as were not quite dead, he set to skin them all.

And ever since then you will observe that the dancers of the Long Horn have blue faces, and whenever they arrive in our pueblo wear collars of coyote-skin about their necks. That is the way they got them. Before that they had no collars. It is presumable that that is the reason why they bellow so and have such hoarse voices, having previously taken cold, everyone of them, for the want of fur collars.

Thus shortens my story.

[1] The *Kâkâ*, or Sacred Drama Dance, is represented by a great variety of masks and costumes worn by Zuñi dancers during the performance of this remarkable dramatic ceremony. Undoubtedly many of the traditional characters of the Sacred Drama thus represented are conventionalizations of the mythic conceptions or personifications of animal attributes. Therefore many of these characters partake at once of the characteristics, in appearance as well as in other ways, of animals and men. The example in point is a good illustration of this. The K'yámakwe are supposed to have been a most wonderful and powerful tribe of demi-gods, inhabiting a great valley and range of mesas some forty miles south of Zuñi. Their powers over the atmospheric phenomena of nature and over all the herbivorous animals are supposed to have been absolute. Their attitude toward man was at times inimical, at times friendly or beneficent. Such a relationship, controlled simply by either laudatory or propitiatory worship, was supposed to hold spiritually, still, between these and other beings represented in the Sacred Drama and men. It is believed that through the power of breath communicated by these ancient gods to men, from one man to another man, and thus from generation to generation, an actual connection has been kept up between initiated members of the *Kâkâ* drama and these original demigod characters which it

represents; so that when a member is properly dressed in the costume of any one of these characters, a ceremony (the description of which is too long for insertion here) accompanying the putting on of the mask is supposed not only to place him *en rapport* spiritually with the character he represents, but even to possess him with the spirit of that character or demi-god. He is, therefore, so long as he remains disguised as one of these demi-gods, treated as if he were actually that being which he personates. One of the K'yámakwe is represented by means of a mask, round and smooth-headed, with little black eyes turned up at the corners so as to represent a segment of a diminishing spiral; the color of the face is green, and it is separated from the rest of the head by a line composed of alternate blocks of black and yellow; the crown and back of the head are snow-white; and the ears are pendent and conical in shape, being composed of husks or other paper-like material; the mouth is round, and furnished with a four-pointed beak of husks, which extends two or three inches outward and spreads at the end like the petals of a half-closed lily; round the neck is a collar of fox fur, and covering the body are flowing robes of sacred embroidered mantles, which (notwithstanding the gay ornaments and other appurtenances of the costume) have, in connection with the expression of the mask, a spectral effect; the feet are encased in brilliantly painted moccasins, of archaic form, and the wrists laden with shell bracelets and bowguards. When the long file of these strange figures making up the

K'yámakwe Drama Dance comes in from the southward to the dance plazas of the pueblo, each member of it bears on his back freshly slain deer, antelope, rabbits, and other game animals or portions of them in abundance, made up in packages, highly decorated with tufts of evergreen, and painted toys for presentation to the children. In one hand are carried bows and arrows, and in the other a peculiar rattle or clanger made of the shoulder-blades of deer. The wonder expressed by the coyote as the story goes on, and his excessive admiration of the children of the K'yámakwe may therefore be understood.

 The Coyote and the Beetle

*I*n remote times, after our ancients were settled at Middle Ant Hill, a little thing occurred which will explain a great deal.

My children, you have doubtless seen Tip-beetles. They run around on smooth, hard patches of ground in spring time and early summer, kicking their heels into the air and thrusting their heads into any crack or hole they find.

Well, in ancient times, on the pathway leading around to Fat Mountain, there was one of these Beetles running about in all directions in the sunshine, when a Coyote came trotting along. He pricked up his ears, lowered his nose, arched his neck, and stuck out his paw toward the Beetle. "Ha!" said he, "I shall bite you!"

The Beetle immediately stuck his head down close to the ground, and lifting one of his antennae deprecatingly, exclaimed: "Hold on! Hold on, friend! Wait a bit, for the love of mercy! I hear something very strange down below here!"

"Humph!" replied the Coyote. "What do you hear?"

"Hush! Hush!" cried the Beetle, with his head still to the ground. "Listen!"

So the Coyote drew back and listened most attentively. By-and-by the Beetle lifted himself with a long sigh of relief.

"*Okwe!*" exclaimed the Coyote. "What was going on?"

"The Good Soul save us!" exclaimed the Beetle, with a shake of his head. "I heard them saying down there that tomorrow they would chase away and thoroughly chastise everybody who defiled the public trails of this country, and they are making ready as fast as they can!"

"Souls of my ancestors!" cried the Coyote. "I have been loitering along this trail this very morning, and have defiled it repeatedly. I'll cut!" And away he ran as fast as he could go.

The Beetle, in pure exuberance of spirits, turned somersaults and stuck his head in the sand until it was quite turned.

Thus did the Beetle in the days of ancients save himself from being bitten. Consequently the Tip-beetle has that strange habit of kicking his heels into the air and sticking his head in the sand.

Thus shortens my story.

How the Coyote Danced

with the Blackbirds

One late autumn day in the times of the ancients, a large council of Blackbirds were gathered, fluttering and chattering, on the smooth, rocky slopes of Gorge Mountain, northwest of Zuñi. Like ourselves, these birds, as you are well aware, congregate together in autumn time, when the harvests are ripe, to indulge in their festivities before going into winter quarters; only we do not move away, while they, on strong wings and swift, retreat for a time to the Land of Everlasting Summer.

Well, on this particular morning they were making a great noise and having a grand dance, and this was the way of it: They would gather in one vast flock, somewhat orderly in its disposition, on the sloping face of Gorge Mountain—the older birds in front, the younger ones behind—and down the slope, chirping and fluttering, they would hop, hop, hop, singing:

Ketchu, Ketchu, oñtilã, oñtilã,
Ketchu, Ketchu, oñtilã, oñtilã!
   Ashokta a yá-à-laa Ke-e-tchu,
     Oñtilã,
     Oñtilã!—
Blackbirds, Blackbirds, dance away, O, dance away, O!
Blackbirds, Blackbirds, dance away, O, dance away, O!
   Down the Mountain of the Gorges, Blackbirds,
     Dance away, O!
     Dance away, O!—

and, spreading their wings, with many a flutter, flurry, and scurry, *keh keh—keh keh—keh keh—keh keh*—they would fly away into the air, swirling off in a dense, black flock, circling far upward and onward; then, wheeling about and darting down, they would dip themselves in the broad spring which flows out at the foot of the mountain, and return to their dancing place on the rocky slopes.

A Coyote was out hunting (as if he could catch anything, the beast!) and saw them, and was enraptured.

"You beautiful creatures!" he exclaimed. "You graceful dancers! Delight of my senses! How do you do that, anyway?

Couldn't I join in your dance—the first part of it, at least?"

"Why, certainly; yes," said the Blackbirds. "We are quite willing," the masters of the ceremony said.

"Well," said the Coyote, "I can get on the slope of the rocks and I can sing the song with you; but I suppose that when you leap off into the air I shall have to sit there patting the rock with my paw and my tail and singing while you have the fun of it."

"It may be," said an old Blackbird, "that we can fit you out so that you can fly with us."

"Is it possible!" cried the Coyote, "Then by all means do so. By the Blessed Immortals! Now if I am only able to circle off into the air like you fellows, I'll be the biggest Coyote in the world!"

"I think it will be easy," resumed the old Blackbird. "My children," said he, "you are many, and many are your wing-feathers. Contribute each one of you a feather to our friend." Thereupon the Blackbirds, each one of them, plucked a feather from his wing. Unfortunately they all plucked feathers from the wings on the same side.

"Are you sure, my friend," continued the old Blackbird, "that you are willing to go through the operation of having these feathers planted in your skin? If so, I think we can fit you out."

"Willing?—why, of course I am willing." And the Coyote held up one of his arms, and, sitting down, steadied himself with his tail. Then the Blackbirds thrust in the feathers all along the rear of his forelegs and down the sides of his back, where wings ought to be. It hurt, and the Coyote twitched his mustache considerably; but he said nothing. When it was done, he asked: "Am I ready now?"

"Yes," said the Blackbirds; "we think you'll do."

So they formed themselves again on the upper part of the slope, sang their songs, and hopped along down with many a flutter, flurry, and scurry—*Keh keh, keh keh, keh keh*—and away they flew into the air.

The Coyote, somewhat startled, got out of time, but followed bravely, making heavy flops; but, as I have said before, the wings he was supplied with were composed of feathers all plucked from one side, and therefore he flew slanting and spirally and brought up with a whack, which nearly knocked the breath out of him, against the side of the mountain. He picked himself up, and shook himself, and cried out: "Hold!

Hold! Hold on, hold on, there!" to the fast-disappearing Blackbirds. "You've left me behind!"

When the birds returned they explained: "Your wings are
not quite thick enough, friend; and, besides, even a young
Blackbird, when he is first learning to fly, does just this sort of
thing that you have been doing—makes bad work of it."

"Sit down again," said the old Blackbird. And he called out
to the rest: "Get feathers from your other sides also, and be
careful to select a few strong feathers from the tips of the wings,
for by means of these we cleave the air, guide our movements,
and sustain our flight."

So the Blackbirds all did as they were bidden, and after the
new feathers were planted, each one plucked out a tail-feather,
and the most skillful of the Blackbirds inserted these feathers
into the tip of the Coyote's tail. It made him wince and "yip"
occasionally; but he stood it bravely and reared his head proudly,
thinking all the while: "What a splendid Coyote I shall be! Did
ever anyone hear of a Coyote flying?"

The procession formed again. Down the slope they went,
hopity-hop, hopity-hop, singing their song, and away they flew
into the air, the Coyote in their midst. Far off and high they

circled and circled, the Coyote cutting more eager pranks than any of the rest. Finally they returned, dipped themselves again into the spring, and settled on the slopes of the rocks.

"There, now," cried out the Coyote, with a flutter of his feathery tail, "I can fly as well as the rest of you."

"Indeed, you do well!" exclaimed the Blackbirds. "Shall we try it again?"

"Oh, yes! Oh, yes! I'm a little winded," cried the Coyote, "but this is the best fun I ever had."

The Blackbirds, however, were not satisfied with their companion. They found him less sedate than a dancer out to be, and, moreover, his irregular cuttings-up in the air were not to their taste. So the old ones whispered to one another: "This fellow is a fool, and we must pluck him when he gets into the air. We'll fly so far this time that he will get a little tired out and cry to us for assistance."

The procession formed, and hopity-hop, hopity-hop, down the mountain slope they went, and with many a flutter and flurry flew off into the air. The Coyote, unable to restrain himself, even took the lead. On and on and on they flew, the Blackbirds and the Coyote, and up and up and up, and they circled round and round, until the Coyote found himself missing a wing stroke occasionally and falling out of line; and he cried out: "Help! Help, friends, help!"

"All right!" cried the Blackbirds. "Catch hold of his wings; hold him up!" cried the old ones. And the Blackbirds flew at him; and every time they caught hold of him (the old fool all the time thinking they were helping) they plucked out a feather, until at last the feathers had become so thin that he began to fall, and he fell and fell and fell—flop, flop, flop, he went through the air—the feathers left in his forelegs and sides and the tip of his tail just saving him from being utterly crushed as he fell with a thud to the ground. He lost his senses completely, and lay there as if dead for a long time. When he awoke, he shook his head sadly, and, with a crestfallen countenance and tail dragging between his legs, betook himself to his home over the mountains.

The agony of that fall had been so great and the heat of his exertions so excessive, that the feathers left in his forelegs and tail-tip were all shrivelled up into little ugly black fringes of hair. His descendants were many.

Therefore you will often meet coyotes to this day who have little black fringes along the rear of their forelegs, and the tips of their tails are often black. Thus it was in the days of the ancients.

Thus shortens my story.

*H*ow the Turtle Out Hunting

Duped the Coyote

*I*n the times of the ancients, long, long ago, near the Highflowing River on the Zuñi Mountains, there lived an old Turtle. He went out hunting, one day, and by means of his ingenuity killed a large, fine deer. When he had thrown the deer to the ground, he had no means of skinning it. He sat down and reflected, scratching the lid of his eye with the nail of his hind foot. He concluded he would have to go hunting for a flint-knife; therefore he set forth. He came after a while to a place where old buildings had stood. Then he began to hum an old magic song, such as, it is said, the ancients sung when they hunted for the flint of which to make knives. He sang in this way:

Apatsinan tse wash,
Apatsinan tse wash,
  Tsepa! Tsepa!

which may be translated, not perhaps correctly, but well enough:

 Fire-striking flint-stone, oh, make yourself known!
 Fire-striking flint-stone, oh, make yourself known!
   Magically! Magically!

  As he was thus crawling about and singing, a Coyote running through the woods overheard him. He exclaimed: "Uh! I wonder who is singing and what he is saying. Ah, he is hunting for a flint-knife, is he?—evidently somebody who has killed a deer!" He turned back, and ran over to where the old Turtle was. As he neared him, he cried out: "Halloo, friend! Didn't I hear you singing?"

  "Yes," was the reply of the Turtle.

  "What were you singing?"

  "Nothing in particular."

  "Yes, you were, too. What were you saying?"

  "Nothing in particular, I tell you; at least, nothing that concerns you."

"Yes, you were saying something, and this is what you said." And so the Coyote, who could not sing the song, deliberately repeated the words he had heard.

"Well, suppose I did say so; what of that?" said the Turtle.

"Why, you were hunting for a flint-knife; that is why you said what you did," replied the Coyote.

"Well, what of that?"

"What did you want the flint-knife for?"

"Nothing in particular," replied the Turtle.

"Yes, you did; you wanted it for something. What was it?"

"Nothing in particular, I say," replied the Turtle. "At least, nothing that concerns you."

"Yes, you did want it for something," said the Coyote, "and I know what it was, too."

"Well, what?" asked the Turtle, who was waxing rather angry.

"You wanted it to skin a deer with; that's what you wanted it for. Where is the deer now, come? You have killed a deer and I know it. Tell, where is it."

"Well, it lies over yonder," replied the Turtle.

"Where? Come, let us go; I'll help you skin it."

"I can get along very well without you," replied the Turtle.

"What if I do help you a little? I am very hungry this morning, and would like to lap up the blood."

"Well, then, come along, torment!" replied the Turtle. So, finding a knife, they proceeded to where the deer was lying.

"Let me hold him for you," cried the Coyote. Whereupon he jumped over the deer, spread out its hind legs, and placed a paw on each of them, holding the body open; and thus they began to skin the deer. When they had finished this work, the Coyote turned to the Turtle and asked: "How much of him are you going to give me?"

"The usual parts that fall to anyone who comes along when the hunter is skinning a deer," replied the Turtle.

"What parts?" eagerly asked the Coyote.

"Stomach and liver," replied the Turtle, briefly.

"I won't take that," whined the Coyote. "I want you to give me half of the deer."

"I'll do no such thing," replied the Turtle. "I killed the deer; you only helped to skin him, and you ought to be satisfied with my liberality in giving you the stomach and liver alone. I'll throw in a little fat, to be sure, and some of the intestines; but I'll give you no more."

"Yes, you will, too," snarled the Coyote, showing his teeth.

"Oh, will I?" replied the Turtle, deliberately, hauling in one or two of his flippers.

"Yes, you will; or I'll simply murder you, that's all."

The Turtle immediately pulled his feet, head, and tail in, and cried: "I tell you, I'll give you nothing but the stomach and liver and some of the intestines of this deer!"

"Well, then, I will forthwith kill you!" snapped the Coyote, and he made a grab for the Turtle. *Kopo!* sounded his teeth as they struck on the hard shell of the Turtle; and, bite as he would, the Turtle simply slipped out of his mouth every time he grabbed him. He rolled the Turtle over and over to find a good place for biting, and held him between his paws as if he were a bone, and gnawed at him; but, do his best, *kopo, kopo!* his teeth kept off the Turtle's hard shell. At last he exclaimed, rather hotly: "There's more than one way of killing a beast like you!" So he set the Turtle up on end, and, catching up a quantity of sand, stuffed it into the hole where the Turtle's head had disappeared and tapped it well down with a stick until he had completely filled the crevice. "There, now," he exclaimed, with a snicker of delight. "I think I have fixed you now, old Hardshell, and served you right, too, you old stingy-box!"—whereupon he whisked away to the meat.

The Turtle considered it best to die, as it were; but he listened intently to what was going on. The Coyote cut up the deer and made a package of him in his own skin. Then he washed the stomach in a neighboring brook and filled it with choppings of the liver and kidneys, and fat stripped from the intestines, and clots of blood, dashing in a few sprigs of herbs here and there. Then, according to the custom of hunters in all times, he dug an oven in the ground and buried the stomach, in order to make a baked blood-pudding of it while he was summoning his family and friends to help him take the meat home.

The Turtle clawed a little of the sand away from his neck and peered out just a trifle. He heard the Coyote grunting as he tried to lift the meat in order to hang it on a branch of a neighboring pine tree. He was just exclaiming: "What a lucky fellow I am to come on that lame, helpless old wretch and get all this meat from him without the trouble of hunting for it, to be sure! Ah, my dear children, my fine old wife, what a feast we will have this day!"—for you know the Coyote had a large family over the way—he was just exclaiming this, I say, when the Turtle cried out, faintly: "*Natipa!*"

"You hard-coated old scoundrel! You ugly, crooked-legged beast! You stingy-box!" snarled the Coyote. "So you are alive, are you?" Dropping the meat, he leaped back to where the Turtle was laying, his head hauled in again, and, jamming every crevice full of sand, made it hard and firm. Then, hitting the Turtle a clip with the tip of his nose, he sent him rolling over and over like a flat, round stone down the slope.

"This is fine treatment to receive from the hands of such a sneaking cur as that," thought the Turtle. "I think I will keep quiet this time and let him do as he pleases. But through my ingenuity I killed the deer, and it may be that through ingenuity I can keep the deer."

So the Turtle kept perfectly dead, to all appearances, and the Coyote, leaving the meat hanging on a low branch of a tree and building a fire over the oven he had excavated, whisked away with his tail in the air to his house just the other side of the mountain.

When he arrived there he cried out: "Wife, wife! Children, children! Come, quick! Great news! Killed an enormous deer today. I have made a blood-pudding in his stomach and buried it. Let us go and have a feast; then you must help me bring the meat home."

Those Coyotes were perfectly wild. The cubs, half-grown, with their tails more like sticks than brushes, trembled from the ends of their toe-nails to the tips of their stick-like tails; and they all set off—the old ones ahead, the young ones following single file—as fast as they could toward the place where the blood-pudding was buried.

Now, as soon as the old Turtle was satisfied that the Coyote had left, he dug the sand out of his collar with his tough claws, and, proceeding to the place where the meat hung, first hauled it up, piece by piece, to the very top of the tree; for Turtles have claws, you know, and can climb, especially if the trunk of the tree leans over, as that one did. Having hauled the meat to the very topmost branches of the tree, and tied it there securely, he descended and went over to where the blood-pudding was buried. He raked the embers away from it and pulled it out; they he dragged it off to a neighboring ant-hill where the red fire-ants were congregated in great numbers. Immediately they began to rush out, smelling the cooked meat, and the Turtle, untying the end of the stomach, chucked as many of the ants as he could into it. Then he dragged the pudding back to the fire and replaced it in the oven, taking care that the coals should not get near it.

He had barely climbed the tree again and nestled himself on his bundle of meat, when along came those eager Coyotes.

Everything stuck up all over them with anxiety for the feast—their hair, the tips of their ears, and the points of their tails; and as they neared the place and smelt the blood and the cooked meat, they began to sing and dance as they came along, and this was what they sang:

Na-ti tsa, na-ti-tsa!
Tui-ya si-si na-ti tsa!
Tui-ya si-si na-ti tsa!
Tui-ya si-si! Tui-ya si-si!

We will have to translate this—which is so old that who can remember exactly what it means?—thus:

Meat of the deer, meat of the deer!
Luscious fruit-like meat of the deer!
Luscious fruit-like meat of the deer!
Luscious fruit-like! Luscious fruit-like!

No sooner had they neared the spot where they smelt the meat than, without looking around at all, they made a bound for it. But the old Coyote grabbed the hindmost of the young ones by the ear until he yelped, shook him, and called out to all the rest: "Look you here! Eat in a decent manner or you will burn your chops off! I stuffed the pudding full of grease, and the moment you puncture it, the grease, being hot, will fly out and burn you. Be careful and dignified, children. There is plenty of time, and you shall be satisfied. Don't gorge at the first helping!"

But the moment the little Coyotes were freed, they made a grand bounce for the tempting stomach, tearing it open, and grabbing huge mouthfuls. It may be surmised that the fire-ants were not comfortable. They ran all over the lips and cheeks of the voracious little gormands and bit them until they cried out, shaking their heads and rubbing them in the sand: "*Atu-tu-tu-tu-tu-tu!*"

"There, now, didn't I tell you, little fools, to be careful? It was the grease that burnt you. Now I hope you know enough to eat a little more moderately. There's plenty of time to satisfy yourselves, I say," cried the old Coyote, sitting down on his haunches.

Then the little cubs and the old woman attacked the delicacy again. "*Atu-tu-tu-tu-tu-tu-tu!*" they exclaimed, shaking their heads and flapping their ears; and presently they all went away and sat down, observing this wonderful hot pudding.[1]

Then the Coyote looked around and observed that the meat was gone, and, following the grease and blood spots up the

tree with his eye, saw in the top the pack of meat with the
Turtle calmly reclining upon it and resting, his head stretched
far out on his hand. The Turtle lifted his head and exclaimed:
"*Pe-sa-las-ta-i-i-i-i!*"

"You tough-hided old beast!" yelled the Coyote, in an
ecstasy of rage and disappointment. "Throw down some of that
meat, now, will you? I killed that deer; you only helped me skin
him; and here you have stolen all the meat. Wife! Children!
Didn't I kill the deer?" he cried, turning to the rest.

"Certainly you did, and he's a sneaking old wretch to steal
it from you!" they exclaimed in chorus, looking longingly at the
pack of meat in the top of the tree.

"Who said I stole the meat from you?" cried out the Turtle.
"I only hauled it up here to keep it from being stolen, you
villain! Scatter yourselves out to catch some of it. I will throw as
fine a pair of ribs down to you as ever you saw. There, now,
spread yourselves out and get close together. Ready?" he called,
as the Coyotes lay down on their backs side by side and
stretched their paws as high as they could eagerly and
tremblingly toward the meat.

"Yes, yes!" cried the Coyotes, in one voice. "We are all
ready! Now, then!"

The old Turtle took up the pair of ribs, and, catching them in his beak, crawled to the end of the branch immediately over the Coyotes, and, giving them a good fling, dropped them as hard as he could. Over and over they fell, and then came down like a pair of stones across the bodies of the Coyotes, crushing the wind out of them, so that they had no breath left with which to cry out, and most of them were instantly killed. But the two little cubs at either side escaped with only a hurt or two, and, after yelling fearfully, one of them took his tail between his legs and ran away. The other one, still very hungry, ran off with his tail lowered and his nose to the ground, sidewise, until he had got to a safe distance, and then he sat down and looked up. Presently he thought he would return and eat some of the meat from the ribs.

"Wait!" cried the old Turtle, "don't go near that meat; leave it alone for your parents and brothers and sisters. Really, I am so old and stiff that it took me a long time to get out to the end of that limb, and I am afraid they went to sleep while I was getting there, for see how still they lie."

"By my ancestors!" exclaimed the Coyote, looking at them; "that is so."

"Why don't you come up here and have a feast with me,"

said the Turtle, "and leave that meat alone for your brothers and sisters and your old ones?"

"How can I get up there?" whined the Coyote, crawling nearer to the tree.

"Simply reach up until you get your paw over one of the branches, and then haul yourself up," replied the Turtle.

The little Coyote stretched and jumped, and, though he sometimes succeeded in getting his paw over the branch, he fell back, *flop!* every time. And then he would yelp and sing out as though every bone in his body was broken.

"Never mind! never mind!" cried the Turtle. "I'll come down and help you." So he crawled down the tree, and, reaching over, grabbed the little Coyote by the topknot, and by much struggling he was able to climb up. When they got to the top of the tree the Turtle said: "There, now, help yourself."

The little Coyote fell to and filled himself so full that he was a round as a plum and elastic as a cranberry. Then he looked about and licked his chops and tried to breathe, but couldn't more than half, and said: "Oh, my! if I don't get some water I'll choke!"

"My friend," said the Turtle, "do you see that drop of water gleaming in the sun at the end of that branch of this pine tree?

(It was really pitch.) "Now, I have lived in the tops of trees so much that I know where to go. Trees have springs. Look at that."

The Coyote looked and was convinced.

"Walk out, now, to the end of the branch, or until you come to one of those drops of water, then take it in your mouth and suck, and all the water you want will flow out."

The little Coyote started. He trembled and was unsteady on his legs, but managed to get half way. "Is it here?" he called, turning round and looking back.

"No, a little farther," said the Turtle.

So he cautiously stepped a little farther. The branch was swaying dreadfully. He turned his head, and just as he was saying, "Is it here?" he lost his balance and fell plump to the ground, striking so hard on the tough earth that he was instantly killed.

"There, you wretched beast!" said the old Turtle with a sigh of relief and satisfaction. "Ingenuity enabled me to kill a deer. Ingenuity enabled me to retain the deer."

It must not be forgotten that one of the little Coyotes ran away. He had numerous descendants, and ever since that time they have been characterized by pimples all over their faces where the mustaches grow out, and little blotches inside of their lips, such as you see inside the lips of dogs.

Thus shortens my story.

NOTE

[1] It may be well to explain here that there is no more intensely painful or fiery bite known than the bite of the fire-ant or red ant of the Southwest and the tropics, named, in Zuñi, *halo*. Large pimples and blisters are raised by the bite, which is so venomous, moreover, that for the time being it poisons the blood and fills every vein of the body with burning sensations.

The Coyote and the Locust

*I*n the days of the ancients, there lived south of Zuñi, beyond the headland of rocks, at a place called Suski-ashokton ("Rock Hollow of the Coyotes"), an old Coyote. And this side of the headland of rocks, in the bank of a steep arroyo, lived an old Locust, near where stood a piñon tree, crooked and so bereft of needles that it was sunny.

One day the Coyote went out hunting, leaving his large family of children and his old wife at home. It was a fine day and the sun was shining brightly, and the old Locust crawled out of his home in the loam of the arroyo and ascended to one of the bare branches of the piñon tree, where, hooking his feet firmly into the bark, he began to sing and play his flute. The Coyote in his wanderings came along just as he began to sing these words:

Tchumali, tchumali, shohkoya,
Tchumali, tchumali, shohkoya!
  Yaamii heeshoo taatani tchupatchinte,
    Shohkoya,
    Shohkoya!

Locust, locust, playing a flute,
Locust, locust, playing a flute!
  Away up above on the pine-tree bough,
    closely clinging,
      Playing a flute,
      Playing a flute!

"Delight of my senses!" called out the Coyote squatting down on his haunches and looking up, with his ears pricked and his mouth grinning. "Delight of my senses, how finely you play your flute!"

"Do you think so?" said the Locust, continuing his song.

"Goodness, yes!" cried the Coyote, shifting nearer. "What a song it is! Pray, teach it to me, so that I can take it home and dance my children to it. I have a large family at home."

"All right," said the Locust. "Listen, then." And he sang his song again:

Tchumali, tchumali, shohkoya,
Tchumali, tchumali, shohkoya!
 Yaamii heeshoo taatani tchupatchinte,
  Shohkoya,
  Shohkoya!

"Delightful!" cried the Coyote. "Now, shall I try?"

"Yes, try."

Then in a very hoarse voice the Coyote half growled and half sang (making a mistake here and there, to be sure) what the Locust had sung, though there was very little music in his repetition of the performance.

Tchu u-mali, tchumali—shohshoh koya,
Tchu tchu mali, tchumali shohkoya,
 Yaa mami he he shoo ta ta tante tchup patchin te,
  Shohkoya,
  Shohkoya!

"Ha!" laughed he, as he finished; "I have got it, haven't I?"

"Well, yes," said the Locust, "fairly well."

"Now, then, let us sing it over together."

And while the Locust piped shrilly the Coyote sang gruffly, though much better than at first, the song.

"There, now," exclaimed he, with a whisk of his tail, "didn't I tell you?" and without waiting to say another word he whisked away toward his home beyond the headland of rocks. As he was running along the plain he kept repeating the song to himself, so that he would not forget it, casting his eyes into the air, after the manner of men in trying to remember or to say particularly fine things, so that he did not notice on old Gopher peering at him somewhat ahead on the trail; and the old Gopher laid a trap for him in his hole.

The Coyote came trotting along, singing: "*Shohkoya, shohkoya,*" when suddenly he tumbled heels over head into the Gopher's hole. He sneezed, began to cough, and to rub the sand out of his eyes; and then jumping out, cursed the Gopher heartily, and tried to recall his song, but found that he had utterly forgotten it, so startled had he been.

"The lubber-cheeked old Gopher! I wish the pests were all in the Land of Demons!" cried he. "They dig their holes, and nobody can go anywhere in safety. And now I have forgotten my song. Well, I will run back and get the old Locust to sing it over again. If he can sit there singing to himself, why can't he sing it to me? No doubt in the world he is still out there on that piñon branch singing away." Saying which, he ran back as fast as he could. When he arrived at the piñon tree, sure enough, there was the old Locust still sitting and singing.

"Now, how lucky this is, my friend!" cried the Coyote, long before he had reached the place. "The lubber-cheeked, fat-sided old Gopher dug a hole right in my path; and I went along singing your delightful song and was so busy with it that I fell headlong into the trap he had set for me, and I was so startled that, on my word, I forgot all about the song, and I have come back to ask you to sing it for me again."

"Very well," said the Locust. "Be more careful this time." So he sang the song over.

"Good! Surely I'll not forget it this time," cried the Coyote; so he whisked about, and away he sped toward his home beyond the headland of rocks. "Goodness!" said he to himself, as he went along; "what a fine thing this will be for my children! How they will be quieted by it when I dance them as I sing it! Let's see how it runs. Oh, yes!

> *Tchumali, tchumali, shohkoya,*
> *Tchumali, tchumali, shohko—*

Thli-i-i-i-p, piu-piu, piu-piu! fluttered a flock of Pigeons out of the bushes at his very feet, with such a whizzing and whistling that the Coyote nearly tumbled over with fright, and, recovering himself, cursed the Doves heartily, calling them "gray-backed, useless sage-vermin"; and, between his fright and his anger, was so much shaken up that he again forgot his song.

Now, the Locust wisely concluded that his would be the case, and as he did not like the Coyote very well, having been told that sometimes members of his tribe were by no means friendly to Locusts and other insects, he concluded to play him a trick and teach him a lesson in the minding of his own affairs. So, catching tight hold of the bark, he swelled himself up and strained until his back split open; then he skinned himself out of his old skin, and, crawling down the tree, found a suitable quartz stone, which, being light-colored and clear, would not make his skin look unlike himself. He took the stone up the tree and carefully placed it in the empty skin. Then he cemented the back together with a little pitch and left his exact counterfeit sticking to the bark, after which he flew away to a neighboring tree.

No sooner had the Coyote recovered his equanimity to some extent than, discovering the loss of his song and again exclaiming "No doubt he is still there piping away; I'll go and get him to sing it over"—he ran back as fast as he could.

"Ah wha!" he exclaimed, as he neared the tree. "I am quite fatigued with all this extra running about. But, no matter; I see you are still there, my friend. A lot of miserable, gray-backed Ground-pigeons flew up right from under me as I was going along singing my song, and they startled me so that I forgot it; but I tell you, I cursed them heartily! Now, my friend, will you not be good enough to sing once more for me?"

He paused for a reply. None came.

"Why, what's the matter? Don't you hear me?" yelled the Coyote, running nearer, looking closely, and scrutinizing the Locust. "I say, I have lost my song, and want you to sing for me again. Will you, or will you not?" Then he paused.

"Look here, are you going to sing for me or not?" continued the coyote, getting angry.

No reply.

The Coyote stretched out his nose, wrinkled up his lips, and snarled: "Look here, do you see my teeth? Well, I'll ask you just four times more to sing for me, and if you don't sing then, I'll snap you up in a hurry, I tell you. Will—you—sing—for me? Once. Will you sing—for me? Twice. Two more times! Look out! Will you sing for me? Are you a fool? Do you see my teeth? Only once more! Will—you—sing—for me?"

No reply.

"Well, you are a fool!" yelled the Coyote, unable to restrain himself longer, and making a quick jump, he snapped the Locust skin off of the bough, and bit it so hard that it crushed and broke the teeth in the middle of his jaw, driving some of them so far down in his gums that you could hardly see them, and crowding the others out so that they were regular tusks. The Coyote dropped the stone, rolled in the sand, and howled and snarled and wriggled with pain. Then he got up and shook his head, and ran away with his tail between his legs. So excessive was his pain that at the first brook he came to he stooped down to lap up water in order to alleviate it, and he there beheld what you and I see in the mouths of every Coyote we ever catch—that the teeth back of the canines are all driven down, so that you can see only the points of them, and look very much broken up.

In the days of the ancients the Coyote minded not his own business and restrained not his anger. So he bit a Locust that was only the skin of one with a stone inside. And all his descendants have inherited his broken teeth. And so also to this day, when Locusts venture out on a sunny morning to sing a song, it is not infrequently their custom to protect themselves from the consequences of attracting too much attention by skinning themselves and leaving their counterparts on the trees.

Thus shortens my story.

The Coyote and the Ravens Who

Raced Their Eyes

*L*ong, long ago, in the days of the ancients, there lived in Hómaiakwin, or the Cañon of the Cedars, a Coyote—doubtless the same one I have told you of as having made friends with the Woodpounder bird. As you know, this cañon in which he lived is below the high eastern cliff of Face Mountain.

This Coyote was out walking one day. On leaving his house he had said that he was going hunting; but—miserable fellow!—who ever knew a Coyote to catch anything, unless it was a prairie-dog or a wood-rat or a locust or something of the kind? So you may depend upon it he was out walking; that is, wandering around to see what he could see.

He crossed over the valley northward, with his tail dragging along in an indifferent sort of a way, until he came to the place on Thunder Mountain called Shoton-pia ("Where the Shell Breastplate Hangs"). He climbed up the foot-hills, and along the terraces at the base of the cliff, and thus happened to get toward the southeastern corner of the mountain. There is a little column of rock with a round top to it standing there, as you know, to this day.

Now, on the top of this standing rock sat two old Ravens, racing their eyes. One of them would settle himself down on the rock and point with his beak straight off across the valley to some pinnacle in the cliffs of the opposite mesa. Then he would say to his companion, without turning his head at all: "You see that rock yonder? Well, ahem! Standing rock yonder, round you, go ye my eyes and come back." Then he would lower his head, stiffen his neck, squeeze his eyelids, and "*Pop!*" he would say as his eyes flew out of their sockets, and sailed away toward the rock like two streaks of lightning, reaching which they would go round it, and come back toward the Raven; and as they were coming back, he would swell up his throat and say "*Whu-u-u-u-u-u-u*—whereupon his eyes would slide with a *k'othlo!* into their sockets again. Then he would turn toward his companion, and swelling up his throat still more, and ducking his head just as if he were trying to vomit his own neck, he would laugh inordinately; and the other would laugh with him, bristling up all the feathers on his body.

Then the other one would settle himself, and say: "Ah, I'll better you! You see that rock away yonder?" Then he would begin to squeeze his eyelids, and *thlut!* his eyes would fly out of their sockets and away across the mesa and round the rock he had named; and as they flew back, he would lower himself, and say "*Whu-u-u-u-u-u-u,*" when *k'othlo!* the eyes would slide into their sockets again. Then, as much amused as ever, the Ravens would laugh at one another again.

Now, the Coyote heard the Ravens humming their eyes back into their sockets; and the sound they made, as well as the way they laughed so heartily, exceedingly pleased him, so that he stuck his tail up very straight and laughed merely from seeing them laugh. Presently he could contain himself no longer. "Friends," he cried, in a shreiky little voice, "I say, friends, how do you do, and what are you doing?"

The Ravens looked down, and when they saw the Coyote they laughed and punched one another with their wings and cried out to him: "Bless you! Glad to see you come!"

"What is it you are doing?" asked he. "By the daylight of the gods, it is funny, whatever it is!" And he whisked his tail and laughed, as he said this, drawing nearer to the Ravens.

"Why, we are racing our eyes," said the older of the two Ravens. "Didn't you ever see anyone race his eyes before?"

"Good demons, no!" exclaimed the Coyote. "Race your eyes! How in the world do you race your eyes?"

"Why, this way," said one of the Ravens. And he settled himself down. "Do you see that tall rock yonder? Ahem! Well, tall rock, yonder—ye my eyes go round it and return to me!" *K'othlo! K'othlo!* the eyes slipped out of their sockets, and the Raven, holding his head perfectly still, waited, with his upper lids hanging wrinkled on his lower, for the return of the eyes; and as they neared him, he crouched down, swelled up his neck, and exclaimed, "*Whu-u-u-u-u-u.*" *Tsoko!* the eyes flew into their sockets again. Then the Raven turned around and showed his two black bright eyes as good as ever. "There, now! what did I tell you?"

"By the moon!" squeaked the Coyote, and came up nearer still. "How in the world do you do that? It is one of the most wonderful and funny things I ever saw!"

"Well, here, come up close to me," said the Raven, "and I

will show you how it is done." Then the other Raven settled himself down; and *pop!* went his eyes out of their sockets, round a rock still farther away. And as they returned, he exclaimed "*Whu-u-u-u-u-u,*" when *tsoko!* in again they came. And he turned around laughing at the Coyote. "There, now!" said he, "didn't I tell you?"

"By the daylight of the gods! I wish I could do that," said the Coyote. "Suppose I try my eyes?"

"Why, yes, if you like, to be sure!" said the Ravens. "Well, now, do you want to try?"

"Humph! I should say I did," replied the Coyote.

"Well, then, settle down right here on this rock," said the Ravens, making way for him, "and hold your head out toward that rock and say: 'Yonder rock, these my eyes go round it and return to me.'"

"I know! I know! I know!" yelled the Coyote. And he settled himself down, and squeezed and groaned to force his eyes out of his sockets, but they would not go. "Goodness!" said the Coyote, "how can I get my eyes to go out of their sockets?"

"Why, don't you know how?" said the Ravens. "Well, just keep still, and we'll help you; we'll take them out for you."

"All right! All right!" cried the Coyote, unable to repress

his impatience. "Quick! quick! here I am, all ready!" And crouching down, he laid his tail straight out, swelled up his neck, and strained with every muscle to force his eyes out of his head. The Ravens picked them out with a dexterous twist of their beaks in no time, and sent them flying off over the valley. The Coyote yelped a little when they came out, but stood his ground manfully, and cringed down his neck and waited for his eyes to come back.

"Let the fool of a beast go without his eyes," said the Ravens. "He was so very anxious to get rid of them, and do something he had no business with; let him go without them!" Whereupon they flew off across the valley, and caught up his eyes and ate them, and flew on, laughing at the predicament in which they had left the Coyote.

Now, thus the Coyote sat there the proper length of time; then he opened his mouth, and said "*Whu-u-u-u-u-u!*" But he waited in vain for his eyes to come back. And "*Whu-u-u-u-u-u-u-u-u!*" he said again. No use. "Mercy!" exclaimed he, "what can have become of my eyes? Why don't they come back?" After he had waited and "*whu-u-u-u-u-d*" until he was tired, he concluded that his eyes had got lost, and laid his head on his breast, woefully thinking of his misfortune. "How in the world shall I hunt up my eyes?" he groaned, as he lifted himself cautiously (for it must be remembered that he stood on a narrow rock), and tried to look all around; but he couldn't see. Then he began to feel with his paws, one after another, to find the way down; and he slipped and fell, so that nearly all the breath was knocked out of his body. When he had recovered, he picked himself up, and felt and felt along, slowly descending, until he got into the valley.

Now, it happened as he felt his way along with his toes that he came to a wet place in the valley, not far below where the spring of Shuntakaiya flows out from the cliffs above. In feeling his way, his foot happened to strike a yellow cranberry, ripe and soft, but very cold, of course. "Ha!" said he, "lucky fellow, I! Here is one of my eyes." So he picked it up and clapped it into one of his empty sockets; then he peered up to the sky, and the light struck through it. "Didn't I tell you so, old fellow? It is one of your eyes, by the souls of your ancestors!" Then he felt around until he found another cranberry. "Ha!" said he, "and this proves it! Here is the other!" And he clapped that into the other empty socket. He didn't seem to see quite as well as he had seen before, but still the cranberries answered the purpose of eyes exceedingly well, and the poor wretch of a Coyote never knew the difference; only it was observed when he returned to his companions in the Cañon of the Cedars that he had yellow eyes instead of black ones, which everybody knows Coyotes and all other creatures had at first.

Thus it was in the days of the ancients, and hence to this day coyotes have yellow eyes, and are not always quick to see things.

Thus shortens my story.

How the Corn-Pests

Were Ensnared

*I*n the days of the ancients, long, long ago, there lived in our town, which was then called the Middle Ant Hill of the World, a proud maiden, very pretty and very attractive, the daughter of one of the richest men among our people. She had every possession a Zuñi maiden could wish for—blankets and mantles, embroidered dresses and sashes, buckskins and moccasins, turquoise earrings and shell necklaces, bracelets so many you could not count them. She had her father and mother, brothers and sisters, all of whom she loved very much. Why, therefore, should she care for anything else?

There was only one thing to trouble her. Behold! it came of much possession, for she had large corn-fields, so large and so many that those who planted and worked them for her could not look after them properly, and no sooner had the corn ears become full and sweet with the milk of their being than all sorts of animals broke into those fields and pulled down the corn-stalks and ate up the sweet ears of corn. Now, how to remove this difficulty the poor girl did not know.

Yes, now that I think of it, there was another thing that troubled her very much, fully as much as did the corn-pests—pests of another kind, however, for there wasn't an unmarried young man in the all the valley of our ancients who was not running mad over the charms of this girl. Besides all that, not a few of them had an eye on so many possessions, and thought her home wouldn't be an uncomfortable place to live in. So they never gave the poor girl any peace, but hung around her house, and came to visit her father so constantly that at last she determined to put the two pests together and call them one, and thereby get rid, if possible, of one or the other. So, when these young men were very importunate, she would say to them, "Look you! If any one of you will go to my corn-fields, and destroy or scare away, so that they will never come back again, the pests that eat up my corn, him I will marry and cherish, for I shall respect his ability and ingenuity."

The young men tried and tried, but it was of no use. Before long, everybody knew of this singular proposition.

There was a young fellow who lived in one of the outer towns, the poorest of the poor among our people; and not only that, but he was so ugly that no woman would ever look at him without laughing.

Now, there are two kinds of laugh with women. One of them is a very good sort of thing, and makes young men feel happy and conceited. The other kind is somewhat heartier, but makes young men feel depressed and very humble. It need not be asked which kind was laughed by the women when they saw this ugly, ragged, miserable-looking young man. He had bright twinkling eyes, however, and that means more than all else sometimes.

Now, this young man came to hear of what was going on. He had no present to offer the girl, but he admired her as much as—yes, a good deal more than—if he had been the handsomest young man of his time. So just in the way that he was he went to the house of this girl one evening. He was received politely, and it was noticeable to the old folks that the girl seemed rather to like him—just as it is noticeable to you and me today that what people have they prize less than what they have not. The girl placed a tray of bread before the young man and bade him eat; and after he had done, he looked around with his twinkling little eyes. And the old man said, "Let us smoke together." And so they smoked.

By-and-by the old man asked if he were not thinking of something in coming to the house of a stranger. And the young man replied, it was very true; he had thoughts, though he felt ashamed to say it, but he even wished to be accepted as a suitor for his daughter.

The father referred the matter to the girl, and she said she would be very well satisfied; then she took the young man aside and spoke a few words to him—in fact, told him what were the conditions of his becoming her accepted husband. He smiled, and said he would certainly try to the best of his ability, but this was a very hard thing she asked.

"I know it is," said the girl; "that is why I ask it."

Now, the young man left the house forthwith. The next day he very quietly went down into the corn-field belonging to the girl and over toward the northern mesa, for that is where her corn-fields were—lucky being! He dug a great deep pit with a sharp stick and a bone shovel. Now, when he had dug it—very smooth at the sides and top it was—he went to the mountain and got some poles, placing them across the hole, and over these poles he spread earth, and set up corn-stalks just as though no hole had been dug there; then he put some exceedingly tempting bait, plenty of it, over the center of these poles, which were so weak that nobody, however light of foot, could walk over them without breaking through.

Night came on, and you could hear the Coyotes begin to sing; and the whole army of pests—Bears, Badgers, Gophers, all sorts of creatures, as they came down slowly, each one in his own way, from the mountain. The Coyotes first came into the field, being swift of foot; and one of them, nosing around and keeping a sharp lookout for watchers, happened to espy those wonderfully tempting morsels that lay over the hole.

"Ha!" said he (Coyotes don't think much what they are doing) and he gave a leap, when in he went—sticks, dirt, bait, and all—to the bottom of the hole. He picked himself up and rubbed the sand out of his eyes, then began to jump and jump, trying to get out; but it was of no use, and he set up a most doleful howl.

He had just stopped for breath, when a Bear came along. "What in the name of all the devils and witches are you howling so for?" said he. "Where are you?"

The Coyote swallowed his whimpers immediately, set himself up in a careless attitude, and cried out: "Broadfoot, lucky,

lucky, lucky fellow! Did you hear me singing? I am the happiest creature on the face of the earth, or rather under it."

"What about? I shouldn't think you were happy, to judge from your howling."

"Why! Mercy on me!" cried the Coyote, "I was singing for joy."

"How's that?" asked the Bear.

"Why," said the Coyote, "I came along here this evening and by the merest accident fell into this hole. And what do you suppose I found down here? Green-corn, meat, sweet-stuff, and everything a corn-eater could wish for. The only thing I lacked to complete my happiness was someone to enjoy the meal with me. Jump in!—it isn't very deep—and fall to, friend. We'll have a jolly good night of it."

So the old Bear looked down, drew back a minute, hesitated, and then jumped in. When the Bear got down there, the Coyote laid himself back, slapped his thighs, and laughed and laughed and laughed. "Now, get out if you can," said he to the Bear. "You and I are in a pretty mess. I fell in here by accident, it is true, but I would give my teeth and eyes if I could get out again!"

The Bear came very near eating him up, but the Coyote

whispered something in his ear. "Good!" yelled the Bear. "Ha! ha! ha! Excellent idea! Let us sing together. Let them come!"

So they laughed and sang and feasted until they attracted almost every corn-pest in the fields to the spot to see what they were doing. "Keep away, my friends," cried out the Coyote. "No such luck for you. We got here first. Our spoils!"

"Can't I come?" "Can't I come?" cried out one after another.

"Well, yes—no—there may not be enough for you all." "Come on, though; come on! who cares?"—cried out the old Bear. And they rushed in so fast that very soon the pit-hole was almost full of them, scrambling to get ahead of one another, and before they knew their predicament they were already in it. The Coyote laughed, shuffled around, and screamed at the top of his voice; he climbed up over his grandfather the Bear, scrambled through the others, which were snarling and biting each other, and, knowing what he was about, skipped over their backs, out of the hole, and ran away laughing as hard as he could.

Now, the next morning down to the corn-field came the young man. Drawing near to the pit he heard a tremendous racket, and going to the edge and peering in he saw that it was half filled with the pests which had been destroying the corn of the maiden—every kind of creature that had ever meddled with the corn-fields of man, there they were in that deep pit; some of them all tired out, waiting for "the end of their daylight," others still jumping and crawling and falling in their efforts to get out.

"Good! good! my friends," cried the young man. "You must be cold; I'll warm you up a little." So he gathered a quantity of dry wood and threw it into the pit. "Be patient! be patient!" said he. "I hope I don't hurt any of you. It will be all over in a few minutes." Then he lighted the wood and burned the rascals all up. But he noticed the Coyote was not there. "What does it matter?" said he. "One kind of pest a man can fight, but not many."

So he went back to the house of the girl and reported to her what he had done. She was so pleased she hardly knew how to express her gratitude, but said to the young man with a smile on her face and a twinkle in her eye, "Are you quite sure they were all there?"

"Why, they were all there except the Coyote," said the young man, "but I must tell you the truth, and somehow he got out or didn't get in."

"Who cares for a Coyote!" said the girl. "I would much rather marry a man with some ingenuity about him than have all the Coyotes in the world to kill." Whereupon she accepted this very ugly but ingenious young man; and it is notable that ever since then pretty girls care very little how their husbands look, being pretty enough themselves for both. But they like to have them able to think and guess at a way of getting along occasionally. Furthermore, what does a rich girl care for a rich young man? Ever since then, even to this day, as you know, rich girls almost invariably pick out poor young men for their husbands, and rich young men are sure to take a fancy to poor girls.

Thus it was in the days of the ancients. The Coyote got out of the trap that was set for him by the ugly young man. That is the reason why coyotes are so much more abundant than any other corn-pests in the land of Zuñi, and do what you will, they are sure to get away with some of your corn, anyhow.

Thus shortens my story.

*F*RANK HAMILTON CUSHING (1857–1900) began his researches into Native American lifeways at the age of nine, when he began a collection of Indian arrowheads that later became part of the permanent collection of the Smithsonian Institution. At the age of twenty-two, he was hired by Major John Wesley Powell, the famed explorer of the American West, as a field collector for the Bureau of American Ethnology. Powell posted Cushing to Zuñi pueblo, in western New Mexico, where he lived for five years as an honorary member of the Zuñi people. He later served as head of the Hemenway Archaeological Expedition of 1886–88. Among his posthumous publications are *Zuñi Folk Tales* (1981), *Zuñi Breadstuff* (1974), and *Zuñi* (1979).